American Ginseng & Companions

Madison Woods

Wild Ozark™ LLC
https://www.wildozark.com

The mission of Wild Ozark is to bridge the gap between people and the natural world, to help us remember that we are part of a larger whole.

Dedicated to my DRSS

Because he understands my love for the deep, green places

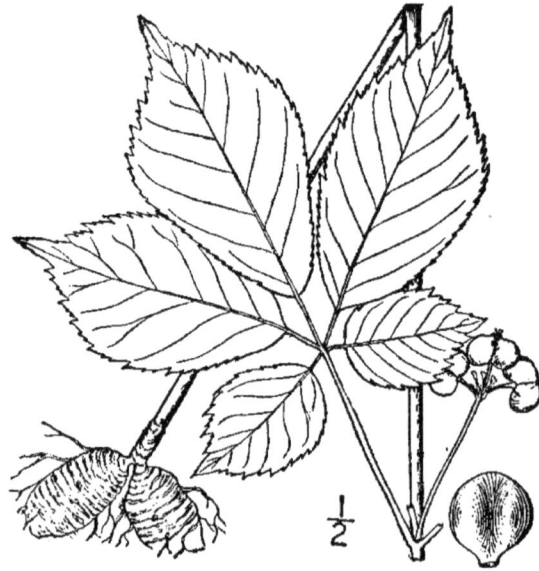

The American ginseng line drawing used throughout this book for chapter and space decoration is from the USDA, NRCS. 2015. The PLANTS Database (http://plants.usda.gov, 5 July 2015). National Plant Data Team, Greensboro, NC 27401-4901 USA.

Table of Contents

Chapter One

Before the Unfurling

The Rousing of Nature

In early spring snow still blankets the ground.

When there is no snow, there is simply cold with an occasional warm day thrown in to tease. Frozen buds patiently await the cue to wake.

The earth slumbers, and yet — if Nature experiences anything like the brainwave patterns of humans, then she is moving into Alpha phase.

She is beginning to stir.

Harbinger of Spring (Erigenia bulbosa)

Sometimes in the wild Ozarks, there's still snow on the ground in early March.

Snow still adorns the usnea moss.

Ice on the rose hips in early March.

Last year's leaves still cling.

In mid-to-late March, the leaves of Adam and Eve orchid appear.

Nature Wakes

One of the first signs that Nature's deep sleep has ended in the rich mixed hardwood forests is the appearance of broad, green, accordion-wrinkled leaves.

Look for the single leaves of Adam and Eve orchids. You'll find them stretched out here and there on the top of dead leaf litter.

Adam and Eve orchid (Aplectrum hyemale)

The flowers of this unusual plant won't bloom until closer to summer. In the meantime, the only greenery it produces is the single leaf.

The plant is also called "putty root", a name harking back to times when village potters played important roles in the community. When the roots were crushed they created sticky goo used by settlers to mend broken pottery.

If you dig up one of these plants you'll see where the other common name is derived. There's always one larger marble-sized root with another smaller pea-sized one attached. The common name is a nod to the Biblical reference of "Adam" and the rib which became "Eve".

Soon the woods are alive with small bits of greenery.

Christmas ferns are still green after the snow has melted. These will soon begin unfurling new fronds, but in the meantime last year's fronds reach for warmth and sunlight.

Grape (Botrychium dissectum, and B. biternatum) and rattlesnake (Botrychium virginianum)

These two ferns are considered "pointer" ferns and old-timers say that they indicate the kinds of habitat preferred by ginseng. A local root digger with many years' experience takes that old saying a step farther. He says the ferns actually point to the ginseng.

Unfortunately, I have not found that to be the case, but the plants really do sometimes grow in the same type of environments. Some of the grape fern leaves can be more cut-leaf than others. Cut-leaf lends a frilly appearance to the fronds. This one is bronzed from being exposed to frost. There's a photo of rattlesnake fern in "bloom" on page 52.

B. biternatum (left) and Botrychium dissectum(right).

Christmas ferns (Polystichum acrostichoides) push back the leaves of winter.

Christmas fern unfurling in early April. Adam and Eve Orchid leaf upper right.

A maple sapling pushes through obstacles and reaches toward light.

Spring Ephemerals

The flowers that bloom in very early spring are fleeting. They provide us with a glimpse of beauty and point our attention toward the ongoing re-emergence of life.

They are the heralds.

Soon the rest of Nature will awaken.

Cutleaf Toothwort (Cardamine concatenate) with closed buds in late March (above) and with open bloom in early April (below).

Bloodroot (Sanguinaria canadensis) begins blooming in late March to early April.

Bloodroot just beginning to bloom while leaves are still clasped.

Rue anemone (Thalictrum thalictroides)

False Rue Anemone (Enemion biternatum)

Round-lobed Hepatica (Anemone americana)

Round-lobed Hepatica (Anemone americana) in purple variation (above) and white (below).

Dutchman's Breeches (Dicentra cucullaria)

Yellow Trout lily flower bud, also called Dog Tooth Violet (Erythronium rostratum)

Ribbons of mist shroud the awakening land.

Chapter Two

The Unfurling

Anticipation

Those of us who haunt the woods to look for certain plants every year wait for spring with the same feeling as waiting for old friends to return from a long trip.

It is a time of impatient anticipation.

My forays into the woods to check for them begin too early, as always, but when the early bloomers finally appear I'm rewarded with preliminary joy.

The photographs in the first chapter captured that initial burst of enthusiasm. Once discovered, the sight of those plants only prompt more frequent jaunts, possibly daily, to watch for the awakening of American ginseng and her close companions.

It is early to mid-April.

Now the unfurling begins.

Three-prong American ginseng (Panax quinquefolius) on the first day above ground. This photo was taken on April 18.

Day 2

Day 3

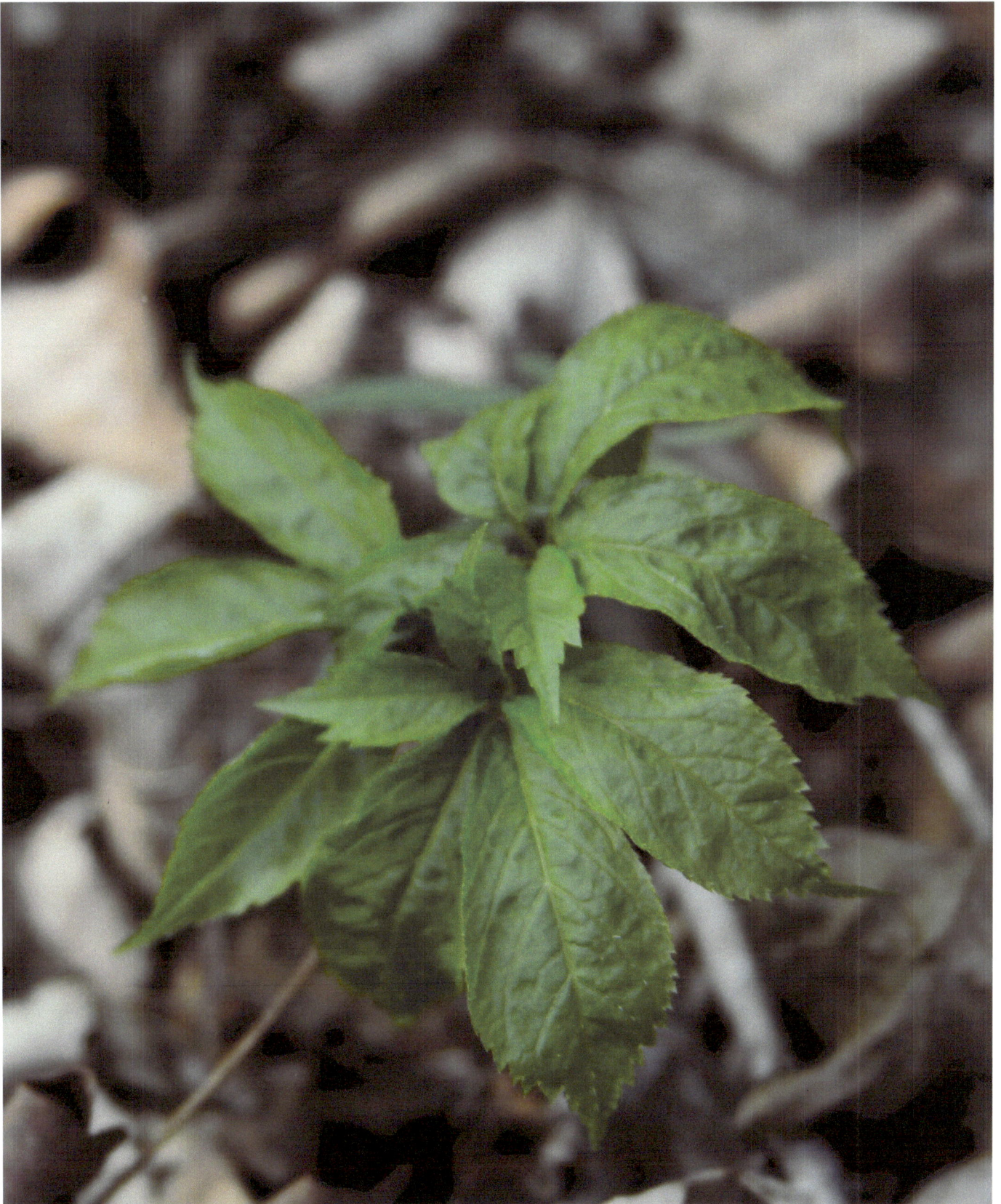

Day four, and this ginseng is nearly finished with the initial stretch. Now it'll continue to grow until flowering in late May to early June.

Look closely. Ginseng is unfurling all around the hillsides now.

Goldenseal (Hydrastis canadensis), one of ginseng's close companions, is also unfurling now.

Goldenseal among trout lily leaves. This two prong goldenseal already has a flower bud.

A three-prong about a week after unfurling.

A three-prong with flower bud at the center, surrounded by immature Jack-in-the-Pulpit.

Two-year old seedlings about a week after unfurling.

The three-prong is at least three years old but could be older. Also in the photo are some first- and second-year seedlings. The plant in the lower left corner is not ginseng.

Woodland Companions

The habitat where ginseng grows is home to other many other plants.

Those that frequently grow in the types of places where ginseng grows are known as "companion plants", or "indicator plants".

The following photographs show some of these companions during the early spring growth phase, through the end of April.

Once the trees have put on leaves, the part of the forest where ginseng habitat occurs is different from the surrounding forest.

The shade is deeper, the air cooler and the ground more moist.

For those attuned to these sorts of variations in nature, there is the distinct feeling of entering a completely different space.

It's like walking into a separate, very special room in a large house.

Blue cohosh (Caulophyllum thalictroides)

Doll's Eye (Actaea pachypoda), also called White Baneberry, in flower.

Goldenseal (Hydrastis Canadensis)

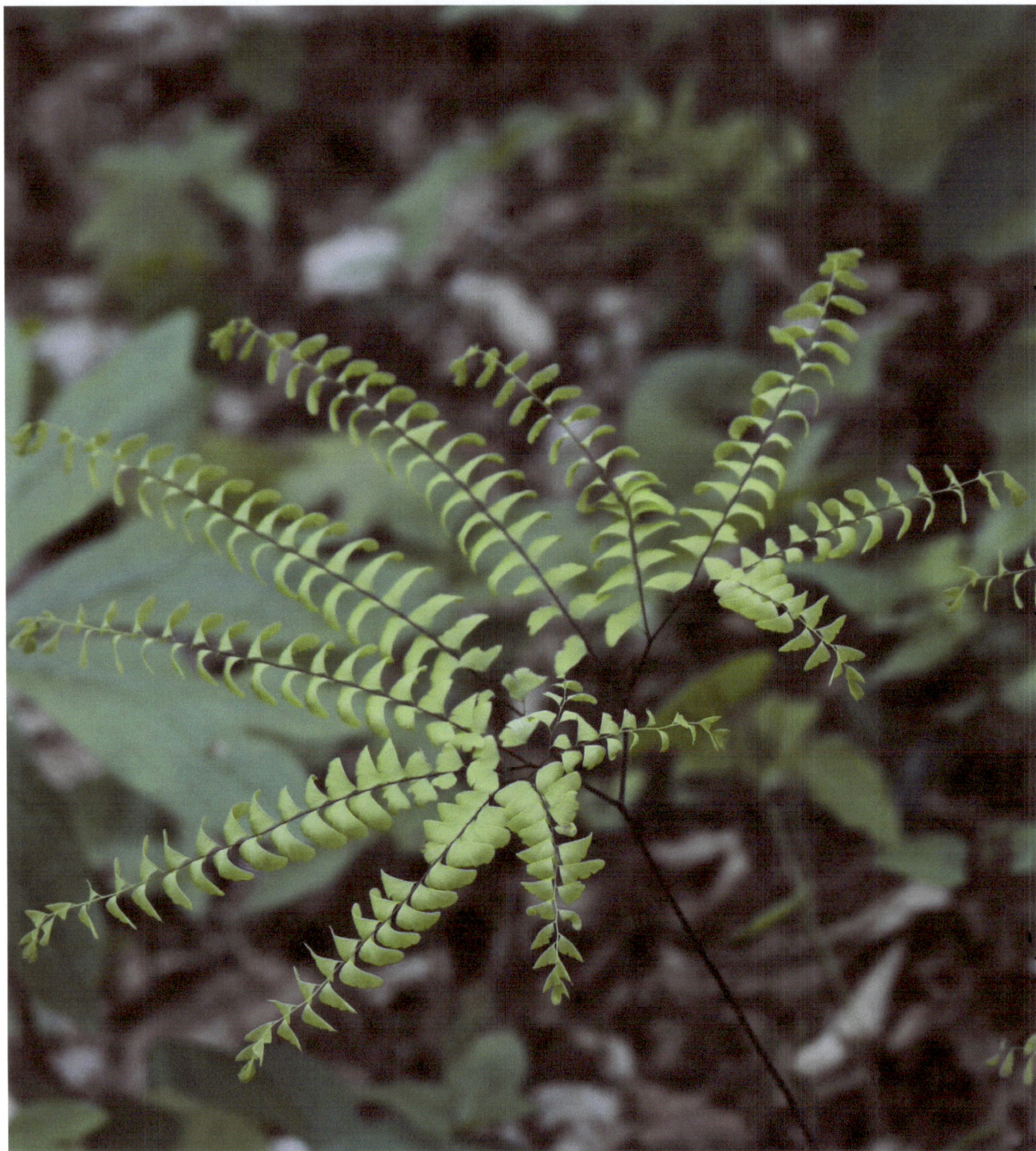

Maidenhair fern (Adiantum pedatum), still unfurling, near the end of April.

Symbiosis in the Forest

Interdependency between circumstances and species is often overlooked by humans, but the perfect alignment of ratios and relationships is what makes the ginseng habitat such a distinct place in space and time.

The ratio between shade and moisture is a crucial relationship, but passive. Plants often grow together in a space because the requirements meet mutual needs, even if they don't need each other. Ginseng and the companion plants enjoy this sort of relationship.

Some species grow together in a habitat because the existence of each are crucial to both. The relationship between plants and fungi is often of this latter sort.

Symbiosis is when the existence and interaction of one life form is necessary for the health and existence of another. Fungi are probably some of the most important inhabitants of this forest.

Fungi go mostly unnoticed, but if you turn over the matted pad of last year's leaves, you'll see the white threads or patches on the ground beneath the leaf cover. That is one part of a network of fungal filaments, mychorrhizial threads, and those are only the ones you can see.

There are many different species and many are invisible to the naked eye. They run behind (or rather, beneath) the scene connecting the entire forest, quietly breaking down nutrients and presenting them to the roots of trees and plants in a form they can use for sustenance, and in return the michorrhizia take sugars from the roots of the trees or plants they support.

Some plants, like the Twayblade Orchid and Maidenhair Fern, need certain fungi present in the soil for their seed or spore to survive and grow into new plants. Many species of fungi associate only with certain species of trees, but some with more than one tree species. This tendency might explain why it's often easier to find morel mushrooms under ash or sycamore trees than other types of trees.

If this topic of the symbiotic relationship between fungi and forest fascinates you, I encourage you to look up "Paul Stametes" in your favorite internet search engine or visit his website at Fungi.com to learn more.

Blossoms of a Dogwood tree (Cornus florida), near the end of April.

Blossoms of a PawPaw tree (Asimina triloba), near the end of April. Later the flowers will open fully and become a deep burgundy red.

Boundaries and Liminal Spaces

There's a "between" space where the ginseng habitat and the surrounding ecosystems meet. It's the boundary between one kind of place and another, like a doorway or threshold.

The ginseng habitat and the surrounding hard wood forest, the forest and the field, or that transition space where mountains meet the ocean, plains, or desert sands — all liminal spaces of a physical sort that speak to the soul of those who enjoy crossing and lingering along such lines.

As we leave the ginseng wood and head toward the field, Pawpaw, Redbud and Dogwood trees mark the line of this particular liminal space.

Redbud Tree (Cercis canadensis)

Maidenhood

If the phases of a woman's life can be called "Maiden", "Mother" and "Crone", then spring to late spring is when Nature can be considered a Maiden.

By the end of April the plants of the ginseng habitat have all unfurled and have begun growing toward fruitfulness.

Insects are attracted to the flowers of the various maidens of the forest and the subsequent fertilization will propel them into the motherhood phase.

The cycle and promise of more new life continues.

Chapter Three

Summer Companions

Full Swing of Summer

If you're looking for the kind of habitat ginseng needs to thrive when seeds or plants are re-introduced, it pays to look for it during summer.

In late spring to early summer, and on through the hottest months the undergrowth and overhead canopies fill in. That is when it's easiest to feel and see the difference between supportive habitat and areas that are too dry, hot, or sunny.

Since ginseng is often difficult to spot if it is there, it's easier to find the companions that mark the magical places.

Many of them grow in conditions too dry or bright for ginseng, but where ginseng grows these also will grow. And where many of the companions are present, odds are good that the conditions are perfect for ginseng as well.

For those interested in restoring a habitat damaged by logging or over-harvesting, getting these plants established should be part of your plan.

If the land was badly damaged and you're trying to restore from scratch, you'll likely also want to plant some of the companion trees: maple, pawpaw, redbud, tulip poplar and beech with a few oaks and hickories to fill in the over-story. Also add shrubs and smaller trees like dogwood, witch hazel and spicebush.

Until the trees get large enough to provide 80% shade during summer, it will be necessary to supplement with man-made shade.

You can do this by attaching shade cloth overhead or building lattice-work at least high enough to be able to walk underneath between the trees.

The following photos show most of the common companions (at least here in the Ozarks) during flowering and fruiting stages.

This large maple tree provides deep shade and creates a perfect ginseng habitat below. Other first-level overstory trees in this habitat include red oak, white oak, tulip poplar and hickory. Smaller trees include redbud, dogwood, and pawpaw. Shrubs provide the third level of overstory and include witch hazel and spicebush.

This Black Cohosh is blooming at the sunny edge of a habitat almost too bright for ginseng.

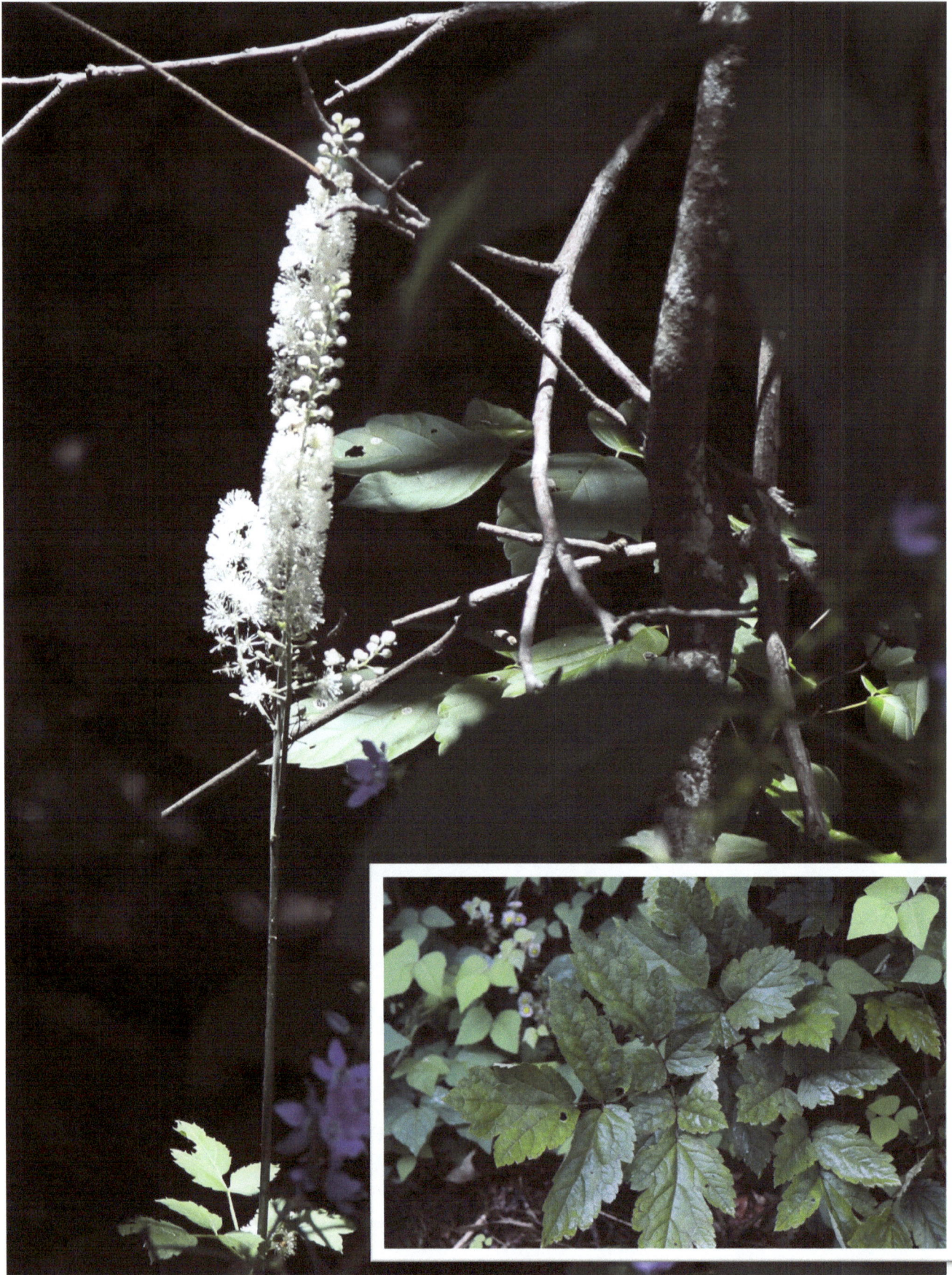

Closer view of the flowers from a plant growing in deeper shade. Inset picture shows the leaves of a Black Cohosh plant.

Doll's Eyes (Actaea pachypoda) are a very frequent close companion. I've only found it in ginseng habitat. Also known as white baneberry, it's very toxic. The plant (but not the flowers and fruit) bears a close resemblance to black cohosh.

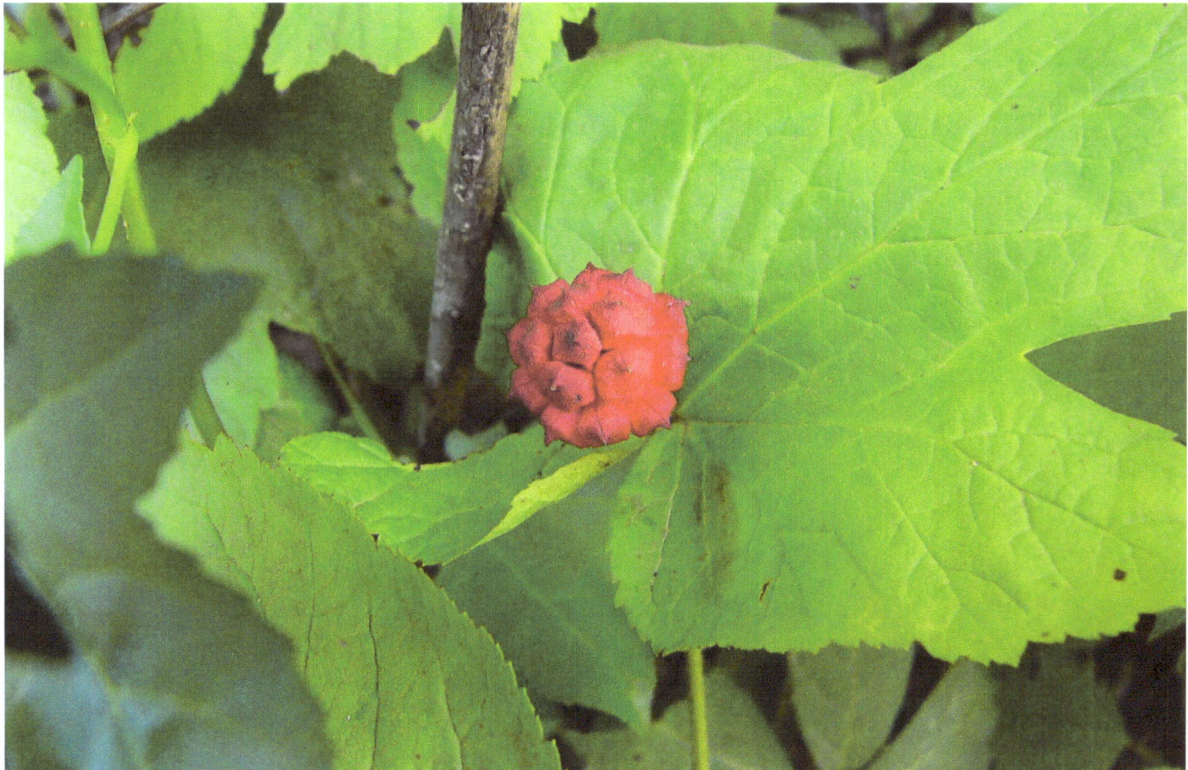

Goldenseal with ripe fruit in June. The root of goldenseal is high in berberine, which gives it the yellow color and medicinal properties.

A bustling family of wild ginger (Asarum canadense). The roots of these plants have a spicy, earthy fragrance.

Christmas fern (Polystichum acrostichoides) is a common companion in the deep shade, but too many will inhibit the growth of other plants.

Above and below: Maidenhair fern (Adiantum pedatum) is at home in the deep shade of a ginseng habitat. The one pictured above is in such deep shade it might be too dark for ginseng.

Rattlesnake fern (Botrichium virginianum) is very similar to grape fern (B. biternatum). Old-timers call them both 'sang pointers, but I've also found them in places ginseng doesn't grow.

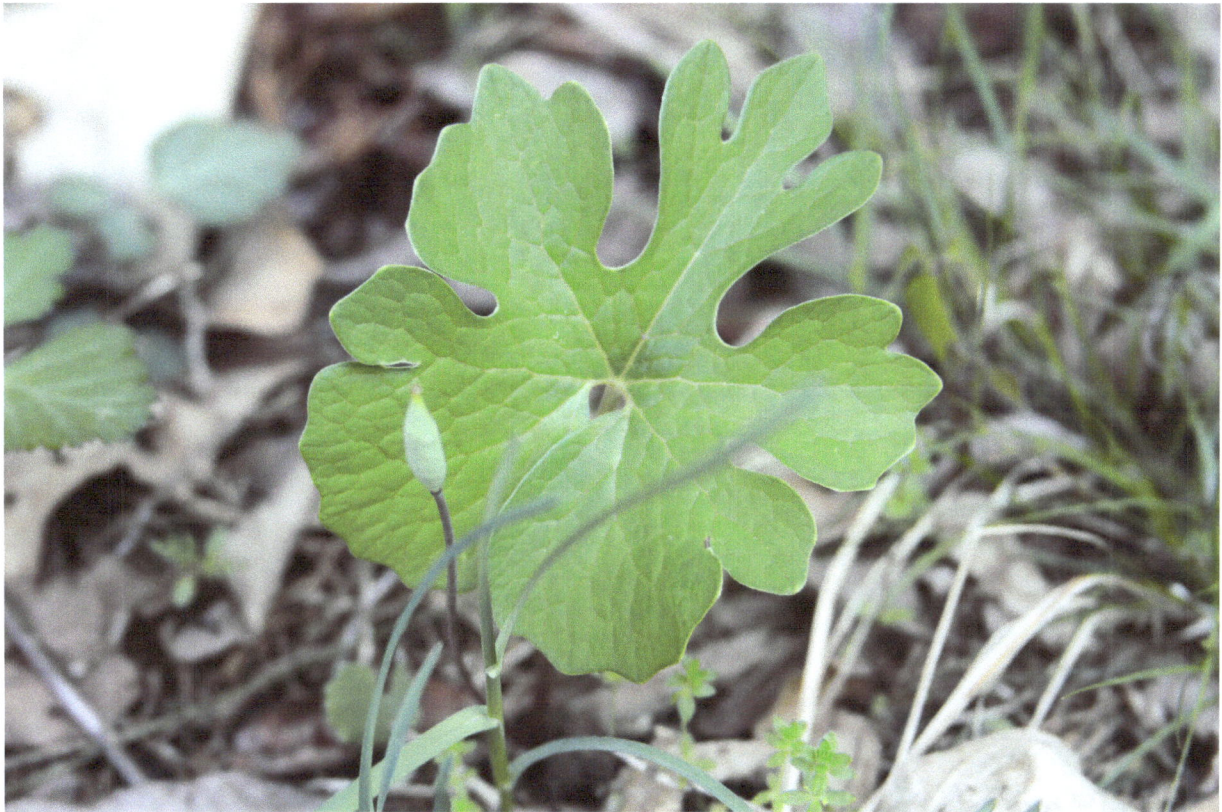

Bloodroot (Sanguinaria candadensis) is finished blooming and seedpods have formed. Below, sap from a broken root "bleeds" bright red.

Above, PawPaw sapling (Asimina triloba). Below left, unripe fruit and right, mature flower.

Photos of American Ginseng

I never tire of looking for ginseng, and the same follows with photographing this elusive plant.

Every single plant inspires me to pull off the lens cap and focus.

It's rare to encounter a thriving colony of even twenty ginseng plants, so each and every one I see in the forest is special.

I suppose if colonies still blanketed the forest floors like it did in the 1700's when explorers first saw them, I might think more of it in terms of group units. But scattered groups of few individuals are all that's left after centuries of decimation.

So I hope you find each and every photo that follows as special as I found the plant that became the subject.

If your property has the right habitat, please consider planting and restoring ginseng and the companion plants if they're not already present.

If wild ginseng is already established on your property and you want to plant more, consider not introducing non-local seeds to the area. The problem of genetic pollution is compounded because it's illegal to buy or sell seeds from wild ginseng. You can, however, plant the seeds from existing wild plants in the same areas of the mother plants.

If you buy seeds, source them from as local as possible and plant these introduced seeds as far from the existing wild colonies as possible.

This author and Mother Earth thank you for caring. Plants don't often get the same concern that endangered animals receive because they just don't inspire the same warm fuzzies the way a gorgeous snow leopard might.

In early May the leaves are sparse on the tree canopy, so more sunlight reaches the ground in the some of the ginseng habitats (above). In other areas, especially those on north-facing slopes, the shade is always fairly dense whether the trees have leafed out or not (below).

Usually by mid-June the berries are plump and green. By mid-July they're beginning to turn red.

In July the berries turn bright red, making it much easier to spot the plants in the woods.

The End is the Beginning

By the end of summer the fruits and berries of the forest companions have all ripened.

The ginseng mother plants still hold a few berries as fall approaches, ready to be planted by diggers and stewards. It's illegal to take the seeds away from the area, so if you encounter any and want to replant (it's the law to replant if you dig), be sure to put them in the ground nearby.

Next year her children and grandchildren will sit at her feet, listening to her for the lore of ginseng.

A mother becomes a crone when she's no longer able to bear children. She enters what is considered the "wisdom" phase of life.

At the end of a season when all the fruit has fallen and stems buckle and break, ginseng goes dormant.

It is during this phase that those nestled in earth's bosom begin to dream and transfer wisdom to the seeds lying beside them.

In spring, the cycle of life begins again.

Chapter Four

The Look-Alikes

Plants that Look Like Ginseng

Even the most seasoned ginseng hunters will sometimes mistake other plants for ginseng at first glance. Here in the Ozarks, the most commonly mistaken plants are Virginia Creeper (*Parthenocissus quinquefolia*), Poison Ivy (*Toxicodendron radicans*), Ohio Buckeye (*Aesculus glabra*), and wild Strawberry (*Fragaria virginiana*).

A 3-prong ginseng (left) next to an Ohio Buckeye (Aesculus glabra) seedling.

Another Ohio Buckeye seedling.

Daddy Long-Legs having lunch on a Poison Ivy (Toxicodendron radicans) leaf.

Virginia Creeper (Parthenocissus quinquefolia).

American ginseng

Virginia Creeper

Wild Strawberry (Fragaria virginiana), above, and ginseng seedlings, below. Notice the hairy stem on the strawberry. Ginseng stems are smooth.

Chapter Five

Resources, Plant List, Closing Notes

Resources

These are the books and websites I use most often in my research of plants:

· Atlas of the Vascular Plants of Arkansas (©2013 Arkansas Vascular Flora Committee)
· USDA Plant Database (http://plants.usda.gov/)
· Arkansas Native Plants (Facebook group)
· Peterson Field Guide to Medicinal Plants and Herbs of Eastern and Central North America
· Plants for a Future (http://www.pfaf.org/)
· United Plant Savers (http://unitedplantsavers.org/)
· Planting the Future, edited by Rosemary Gladstar and Pamela Hirsch

For information on how to use plants or whether they're edible/medicinal I frequent the following books:

· A Modern Herbal by Mrs. M. Grieves (https://www.botanical.com/botanical/mgmh/comindx.html)
· Identifying and Harvesting Edible and Medicinal Plants by Wildman Steve Brill
(http://www.wildmanstevebrill.com/)
· Peterson Field Guide to Medicinal Plants and Herbs of Eastern and Central North America

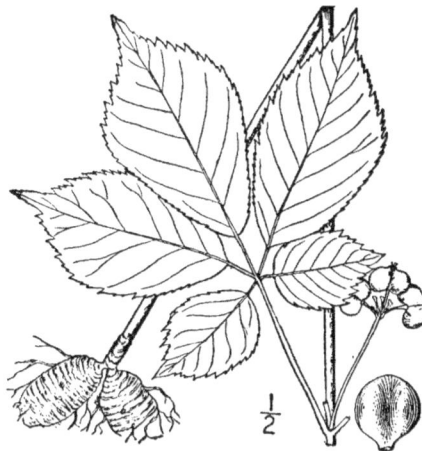

List of Featured Plants

Common and Botanical Names

Adam and Eve Orchid	Aplectrum hyemale
American ginseng	Panax quinquefolius
Black Cohosh	Actaea racemosa
Bloodroot	Sanguinaria canadensis
Blue Cohosh	Caulophyllum thalictroides
Christmas Fern	Polystichum acrostichoides
Cutleaf Toothwort	Cardamine concatenate
Dogwood	Cornus florida
Doll's Eyes	Actaea pachypoda
Dutchman's Breeches	Dicentra cucullaria
False Rue Anemone	Enemion biternatum
Goldenseal	Hydrastis canadensis
Grape Fern	Botrychium biternatum, B. dissectum
Yellow Trout Lily	Erythronium rostratum
Jack-in-the-Pulpit	Arisaema triphyllum
Northern Maidenhair Fern	Adiantum pedatum
Ohio Buckeye	Aesculus glabra
PawPaw tree	Asimina triloba
Poison ivy	Toxicodendron radicans
Rattlesnake Fern	Botrychium virginianum
Round-lobed Hepatica	Anemone americana
Rue Anemone	Thalictrum thalictrocides
Virginia creeper	Parthenocissus quinquefolia
Wild Ginger	Asarum canadense
Wild Strawberry	Fragaria virginiana

This isn't an exhaustive list of all the plants that could appear in a ginseng habitat. Many, such as American Spikenard, are present in some of the habitats, but they're not as common as the ones I've listed, at least not out here in the Ozarks. Blue Cohosh is actually on the "Threatened" list for the state of Arkansas, but I wanted to feature that particular plant mainly because it is on that list.

Depending on where you are, there may be others not mentioned here. I'd to hear from you about it – post a comment to my blog (www.wildozark.com) about the ones you find frequently in your part of the country. There's a link in the menu for "Ginseng". Any of those pages would be a great place to post, but the "Habitat through the Seasons" might be the best.

Closing Notes

Your experience with this book is important to me. Please leave a review at Amazon. I'm always open to praise, criticism or comments and suggestions.

If you'd like a free PDF copy of this book, enter the code below during checkout. Our shop address is https://shop.wildozark.com. You'll find it under the "Books" category.

Coupon code: Am-Ginseng

About Madison Woods

I'm an author/photographer/naturalist with a particular penchant for plants, especially American Ginseng. I live way off the beaten path in northwest Arkansas with my husband, horses, chickens, cats & dogs.

My fiction is usually fantasy with settings or characters influenced by my life in the wild Ozarks, & my nonfiction is usually about the medicinal/edible/useful/beautiful plants I love.

You can find my articles, books, and products at our Wild Ozark's shopping site and my books are also at Amazon.

Feel free to connect with me through any or all of the links below or use any search engine to find me through Wild Ozark:

Email: madison@wildozark.com

My Blog: wildozark.com/madison-woods-blog

Twitter: twitter.com/wildozark

LinkedIn: linkedin.com/in/wildozark

www.ingramcontent.com/pod-product-compliance
Lightning Source LLC
Chambersburg PA
CBHW060820270326
41930CB00003B/100